# HELP IS ON THE WAY FOR:

# Memory Skills

Written by Marilyn Berry
Pictures by Bartholomew

CHILDRENS PRESS ™

CHICAGO

Childrens Press
School and Library Edition

Executive Producers: Ron Berry and Joy Berry
Producer: Ellen Klarberg
Editors: Nancy Cochran and Susan Motycka
Consultants: Kathleen McBride, Maureen Dryden and Donna Fisher
Design: Abigail Johnston
Typesetting: Curt Chelin

Do you sometimes feel that you have to remember too much information?

Hang on! Help is on the way!

If you have a hard time

- remembering information for exams,
- remembering how to spell words, and
- remembering important names, dates, and facts...

...you are not alone!

Just in case you're wondering...

...why don't we start at the beginning?

# What Is Memory?

Memory is a system for people to store and recall information. Every time we learn something, we have the ability to store the information in our brains so that we can use it later.

Memory is very important. Without it, you would have to relearn everything every day. You would not be able to recognize
- sights,
- sounds,
- tastes, or
- smells.

You would not remember anything from the past.

# Two Types of Memory

You have two types of memory: short-term memory and long-term memory. The type of memory you use depends on how long you want to remember the information you are storing.

**Short-term memory** is used when you need or want to remember something only for a short time. This type of information is forgotten within 30 seconds. An example of this is a phone number you seldom use.

**Long-term memory** is used when you need or want to remember something for a longer period of time. This information is reviewed and repeated until it is "memorized" or stored in long-term memory. An example of this is your own telephone number.

# The Importance of Memory Skills

Developing good memory skills is very important. They can make your life easier in many ways. Here are some examples of times when memory skills come in handy:

• Remembering names and faces.

- Remembering important numbers and dates.

- Remembering directions.

Memory skills are also very important for your success in school. You will find that there is information you need to memorize in every subject you study in school. Here are some examples:

• Math

• Spelling

- History

- Geography

13

# Improving Your Memory Skills

No matter how good your memory skills are, there is probably room for improvement. You can improve your memory skills by learning about memory aids and memory tricks. Taking time to do this will make your studying easier and a lot more fun.

## GETTING READY

Before you can successfully memorize something, you must do four important things. You must
- be **interested** in the material,
- **understand** the material,
- **organize** the material, and
- give the material your full **attention.**

**Be Interested.** It is always easier to memorize material if you are interested in it. Try to find something interesting about any material you need to memorize. It will help if you can relate the material to yourself in some way.

**Understand.** It is very difficult to memorize material you don't understand. Before you try to memorize the material
- read through it carefully,
- make a note of anything you do not understand, and
- discuss the material with your teacher until you completely understand it.

**Be Organized.** Most material will be easier to memorize if you organize it. How you organize it depends on the material. Here are two suggestions to keep in mind:

- Divide the material into smaller parts. It will be easier to memorize it one section at a time.
- Put the material in an order that makes sense to you.

**Pay Attention.** You will memorize material faster if you give it your full attention. Do your memorizing in a place with few distractions. It will also help to keep your mind on the material and avoid thinking of other things.

## MEMORY AIDS

There are three memory aids that are an important part of good memory skills. They are calendars, lists, and note cards.

**Calendars.** As you do your schoolwork, there will always be important dates to remember, such as test dates and due dates for assignments. If you keep a calendar, it will help you remember the dates without having to memorize them.

**Lists.** Keeping lists of "things to do" also helps you remember important items without having to memorize them. It is not necessary to memorize such things as homework assignments or a list of needed school supplies. However, it is important that you check your lists every day and remember to do the things on them.

**Note Cards.** When you do need to memorize something, it is a good idea to write the material on note cards. There are some good reasons for this:

- Writing down the material helps you remember it.
- Writing down the material helps you organize it.
- Note cards make great flash cards for studying with others.

# MEMORY TRICKS

There are many tricks you can learn to help you memorize information. Most of them make memorizing fun and easy. It will take some practice to learn how to use these tricks, but it will be worth the effort. These tricks can help you memorize almost anything.

## Visual Images

Visual images are pictures in your mind. Learning how to draw pictures in your mind can help you memorize certain types of information. As you look at a picture in your mind, you need to notice three things:

**Details.** For example, picture a puppy in your mind. Be sure to notice
• what kind of puppy it is,
• what some of its features are, and
• if it has long or short hair.

**Color.** Picture the same puppy. Try to notice
• what color it is,
• if it has any spots, and
• the color of its nose, eyes, and tongue.

**Action.** Picture the same puppy. Have the puppy doing something. The more ridiculous the action, the easier it will be to remember it.

## Visual Image Tricks

There are many ways that visual images can help you memorize. Two fun ways are the link trick and the substitution trick.

**The link trick** is especially useful when you have to memorize a list of items. Here's an example of how it works:

*Step One*

- Think of a word that rhymes with each of the numbers from one to ten. One is a sun, two is a shoe, and so on.
- Write down each number and the word that rhymes with it.
- Go over the list and picture each word in your mind (remember to notice detail, color, and action). Review this list until you know it well. You can use it whenever you need to memorize a list of ten or fewer items.

## Step Two

- Next, write down a second list of words that you need to memorize. For example, let's say you have to memorize a list of five mammals for your science class:

1. a lion
2. a kangaroo
3. a whale
4. a giraffe
5. an elephant

- Link each of the five mammals with an item on your first list and picture them together. Remember to notice detail, color, and action.

- Close your eyes and see if you can remember the list of five mammals. Start with number one. When you picture the sun, what animal do you see?

**Substitution Trick.** Sometimes, you have to remember words that you can't picture in your mind, such as the name of a person or place. In that case, you use substitutes that sound like the words but *can* be pictured. This takes some imagination but it's fun.

"John Adams" might look like this:

"Idaho" might look like this:

## Spy Tricks

There are two memory tricks that will bring out the detective in you. You will be surprised at how clever you can be.

**Hidden Clue Trick.** This trick is especially good for remembering how to spell difficult words.
- Study the word you need to know how to spell.
- Look for a smaller clue word that will help you remember the correct spelling.
- Make up a sentence using both words.

Here are some examples:

''Piece''

"Thorough"

"Business"

**Secret Code Trick.** This trick is another fun way to memorize a list of words.

- Write down the list of words you want to remember.
- Put the words in the order in which you want to memorize them.
- Underline the first letter of each word.
- Make up a sentence using words that begin with same first letters as the words on your list.

An example is a list of the planets in order of their distance from the sun:

If your list of words does not have to be in any special order, you can try something a little different.

- Write down the list of words you want to remember.
- Underline the first letter of each word.
- Try to form a meaningful word out of the letters.

An example is a list of the names of the Great Lakes:

## Creative Tricks

There are several memory tricks that require a little extra creativity. Once your creation is finished, however, you will remember it for a long time.

**Rhyming Tricks.** When you need to memorize important facts, such as historical dates and events, it's a good idea to put these facts into rhyme. You've probably heard, "In 1492 Columbus sailed the ocean blue."

Here's another example:

**Song Tricks.** One of the easiest ways to memorize information is to put it to music. Remember how you learned your ABCs?

- Choose the tune of a very familiar song.
- Organize the information in the order in which you want to memorize it.
- Put the information and the tune together.
- If it doesn't work, try another tune. Remember, it doesn't have to be perfect.

Some of the most important information you will memorize are your multiplication tables. You can make the task easier by putting them to music. Try singing them to the tune of "The Twelve Days of Christmas."

**Game Tricks.** An especially fun way to practice material you need to memorize is to make up games and play them with your friends. Here are two examples:

### Multiplication Dominoes

- Lay all of the dominoes face down on the table.
- One player turns over a domino.
- All players multiply the number on one half of the domino by the number on the other half.
- The first person to call out the correct answer gets a point.
- All other players have to write the multiplication problem and the correct answer on a piece of paper.
- The first player to get twenty points is the winner.

## *States Monopoly*

- On one side of a note card, draw the outline of a state.
- On the other side of the note card, write the name of the state and its capital.
- Do this for all fifty states.
- Put all the cards in a pile with the state outlines face up.
- Player number one tries to identify the state on the top card of the pile.
- If the player is correct, he or she gets to keep the card. If the player can correctly name the state's capital, he or she gets a bonus point.
- If the player is wrong, the card goes on the bottom of the pile, and it is player two's turn.
- When all the cards have been identified, the player with the most cards and bonus points is the winner.

**Rhythm Tricks.** Some information can be easily memorized by putting it to a rhythm. This is similar to doing a cheer. A good example is a word that might be difficult for you to spell.

# Helpful Hints

## Avoid Overloading

Don't try to memorize large amounts of
information in one session. You will remember
more and you will remember it longer if you
review the material in several short sessions.

## Use Your Senses

No matter what kind of memory tricks you use, try to involve as many of these senses as you can:

- Touching—write down the information several times.
- Seeing—read over the information and create visual images.
- Hearing—read the information aloud or read it into a tape recorder and listen to it over and over.

## Review From Time to Time

There will be some information that you will want to remember for a long time. You can keep this information fresh in your memory by reviewing it from time to time.

## Keep Your Note Cards Handy

You never know when you will have a spare minute to review them.

## Practice Your Memory Tricks

The more time you spend practicing your memory tricks, the better your memory skills will become. Work on the tricks that seem difficult. They will become easier with practice.

# WARNING!

If you practice the skills in this book, you'll be amazed at how much information you can memorize...

...and how much fun you had doing it!

**THE END**

## About the Author

Marilyn Berry has a master's degree in education with a specialization in reading. She is on staff as a producer and creator of supplementary materials at the Institute of Living Skills. Marilyn is a published author of books and composer of music for children. She is the mother of two sons, John and Brent.